Hugs & Heartaches

Celebrating the Mysteries of Motherhood

Caroline Ferdinandsen

FAITHFUL Woman

For Her. For God. For Real.
faithfulwoman.com

Faithful Woman is an imprint of
Cook Communications Ministries, Colorado Springs,
Colorado 80918
Cook Communications, Paris, Ontario
Kingsway Communications, Eastbourne, England

HUGS AND HEARTACHES
©2001 by Caroline Ferdinandsen

First Printing, 2001
Printed in the United States of America

1 2 3 4 5 6 7 8 9 10 Printing/Year 05 04 03 02 01

Editor: Sue Reck
Cover Design: Peter Speach, PS Marketing Communications
Interior Design: Scott Johnson, Big Mouth Bass Design, Inc.

Unless otherwise noted, Scripture quotations are taken from
the *King James Version*.

Library of Congress Cataloging-in-Publication Data

Ferdindandsen, Caroline.
    Hugs and heartaches: celebrating the mysteries of
motherhood / Caroline Ferdinandsen.
        p. cm.
     ISBN 0-7814-3476-9
      1. Motherhood. 2. Mothers. I. Title.

    HQ759 .F395 2001
    306.874'3--dc21

                                    00-063636

Table of Contents

❧❧❧

Who else could God possibly use to inspire
these thoughts?

. . . The whispers of three unpredictable little muses

. . . The training of two wise teachers

. . . And the sturdy love of a faithful man named Tye

Acknowledgements

For Sue Reck and Julie Smith: Professional and spiritual insight may be hard to find side by side, but God gave you both. Thanks for helping me land upright.

Preface

In 1994, a pale and messy newborn came squirming into the hands of my obstetrician. My husband and I marveled at God's achievement and we went home to our little house full of gadgets and gifts, ready to start our lives as parents.

We had absolutely no idea.

In the next four years, we had managed to repeat that scenario twice more, and while we now know how to work the gadgets with a bit more dexterity, we still have no idea of the magnitude of our roles as parents.

In that first year, I began a series of observations about my new role as mother. One particular night, after spending several late-night hours conversing with my out-of-town sister, I wrote down a messy page of ideas. On that page were half a dozen paradoxes, seemingly incompatible opposites, that motherhood apparently held. In those early morning hours, the ideas for these chapters were born.

One need only scan the bookshelves to find every type of book written about parenting, and I wonder if mine should join them there. I am not a psychologist, not a public speaker, not a creative writer merely looking for sentimental lines. I am not even a seasoned mother or well-known pastor's wife sharing a lifetime of wisdom.

I am simply a woman whose role as mother has placed me in heaven and earth at the same time. It is a role that is deeply mysterious, yet affords most of us little time to ponder it. But we must. The spiritual nature of motherhood demands that we grapple with it, look at it, turn it over in our hearts, and consider the eternal value of a role that many would dismiss as ordinary. In the late-night hours, after the laundry was folded, the toys returned to their places, and the lullabies gently sung, these chapters afforded me a place to wrestle with the most profound mysteries of motherhood.

Caroline Ferdinandsen

Beacon

This love light blinds me.

I cannot stare into it,
Dim it,
Or stand behind a hill.
I feel warm
Yet sometimes faint
At your arrival.
No chasm,
cave,
or space
Can cloak me in its shadows,
So I lay beneath your light
And let it

Burn.

Chapter One

Eternal Value
and Its Minimum Wage:
The Paradox of a Mother's Work

I was a naïve foreigner in a strange land of pastel gift
wrap, belly patting, and maternity chitchat. I sat
quietly on the sofa at a friend's baby shower, listening to
everything and nothing at the same time. The quiet
buzz, the gentle hum of multiple conversations blending
in the air demanded very little of me. Since I had no
children of my own, I was ill-equipped to share birthing
stories or commiserate about swollen ankles. So there I
sat, observing in silence this wonderful yet mysterious
rite of passage, in which seasoned mothers give gifts and
homespun wisdom to the next woman riding into town.

In between the bits of chatter that faded in and out
of my quiet awareness, two separate conversations
caught my attention. What was most remarkable was not
the subject matter of these conversations, but the irony
of hearing both at the same time.

In one group, several working mothers spoke proud-
ly of their super-mom status, a lifestyle that afforded
them both the financial stability and self-esteem of a
career, together with the domestic joys of cookie baking

and story time. On the other side of the room, another group of women was praising the stay-at-home lifestyle, one that often raises a mother to martyr status and guarantees that her children will emerge more perfect human beings than any deprived day care victims.

As a young woman not yet at the door of motherhood, what was I to think? As I focused in and out of both discussions from a distance, I couldn't help but wonder how the tasks of mothering could take on such different casts and shadows depending on how one held the light.

Ten years and three children later, I've observed that the child care debate between mothers who have a full-time career and those who stay at home to raise their children is still so rhetorical that no one seems to have added anything new to the discussion. The same arguments spin in endless circles. Financial need, availability of two parents, necessity versus choice—certainly each issue is a debate in itself and has prompted plenty of exploration among other writers.

However, one constant seems clear: every woman's natural tendency is to defend her personal choices, straining to work them into scriptural absolutes as she tries to justify her own decisions. We often work backward, choosing our desired path first and then writing our defense strategy later, much like a lawyer hired to protect his client's interests. Even the most self-sacrificing mother has impure motives, given her instinctive pride, given her desire for self-worth, given her humanity.

An Earthly Role

What is at stake in this tired debate is the core issue of a mother's *value*. Any worthwhile discussion of a mother's value must look beyond the world's definitions—and the selfish reasons we depend on them—and into spiritual territory.

We know that a mother's role has eternal value, but do we grasp it? The phrase "eternal value" itself seems like a perfect contradiction in a materialistic society that distorts spiritual reality and strips mothers of their worth. Does this cultural observation naturally condemn the working mother? Certainly not. Does it elevate the stay-at-home mother to sainthood? Doubtful. But it does remind us that the value of our earthly role pays a spiritual—not worldly—wage. We cannot possibly assess our heavenly worth using an earthly formula.

Of course, most discussions of value in our product-oriented society speak numerically, not spiritually. We are obsessed with financial numbers, profit margins, or career output; it seems an individual's value is best revealed through paper and ink. But as with all matters of the spirit, the world and the spirit are bitter enemies. How can it be that in our paradoxical American culture, priceless seems worth very little, and cheap comes with a price?

Our country's mediocre appraisal of its mothers is

not surprising, for while parenting is both earthly and spiritual, surely the earthly tasks are what we experience first. What do we find in a home with young children? Fingerprints. Bodily fluids. Rank diaper pails. Once the lovely newborn cooing has quieted down, a mother begins the blue-collar work of hauling and scraping, disinfecting and grunting. Mothering is messy. Mothering is strenuous. In its most basic human form, mothering is hopelessly mundane. The physical strain of caring for our young bears no resemblance to spiritual matters.

The animal-like tasks I engage in—such as rocking, carrying, suckling, and grooming—seem no different at times from the busy female monkeys at my local zoo. My arms and back seem involved far more often than my soul. Sleep—not spirituality—brings the daily peace I need to survive. While poets, photographers, and our own romantic imaginations produce images of mother and child in graceful poses, they rarely reflect day-to-day parenting during a child's most critical years. It is not that a mother doesn't know her spiritual value; certainly she knows the weight and importance of her moral and spiritual guidance and her indispensable role in preparing young ones for adulthood. It's just that she cannot seem to hear the music of heaven beyond all that crying.

Unnatural Sacrifice

So how do we endure the sacrifices when we lose sight of our spiritual purpose? It never happens all at once. Thankfully, the sacrifices sneak up on us slowly. Pregnancy offers a scientific analogy of how a mother's needs are sacrificed in direct proportion to her child's, as nutrients are automatically transferred from a mother's body to her child's. Natural law reflects what mature mothers already know by instinct: the child's requirements must be satisfied first before consideration is given to his mother.

When a child is born, however, the automatic transfer stops, and now our rights must be relinquished *voluntarily*. We experience sleep deprivation during nighttime feedings. Why? So our babies can sleep better. The same self-control that keeps our anger in check while we discipline is transferred to a child as a result of that discipline. We try to bolster our teenager's self-esteem just at the time when aging robs us of some of our own. *It seems each quality we hope to nurture in our children comes at the expense of our own comfort.* But this is a mother's work, and one who cannot control her own selfish appetite quickly finds she has malnourished children.

What Are We Worth?

In a home with young children, reconciling earthly reality with eternal ideals may seem impossible. The mature mother may instinctively know her children have eternal value. She knows their spiritual growth is critical. She may know every crusty nose and foul diaper is a small sacrifice in the larger scope of eternity. But her spiritual instinct seems silenced by her sinful, pressing need for self-worth. And *self*-worth is so prized by our culture, so idolized by therapists, so coveted by women everywhere that it eventually inhibits our ability to love unconditionally—a wholly divine achievement.

Of course, the Christian's position on self-worth is at odds with our culture. To claim that a mother should deny herself seems so backward, so oppressive. What most fail to realize, however, is that *worth* isn't the issue; *self*-worth is. Self-worth is man-made. It is derived from more superficial desires, such as beauty or popular opinion. It lacks substance or eternal value. Real worth, however, comes from sacrifice. Worth comes from denial. Worth comes from God. Scripture is filled with the paradox of the last becoming first, and like most spiritual concepts, its truth barely penetrates us.

The intimate relationship between the ordinary and the eternal is so unlikely that society rarely recognizes it. It quickly applauds financial profit, athletic skill, entertainment value, external beauty, and youth for their own sakes—all of which are at odds with eternal value. Women are left with the physical indignities of child rearing, realizing of course that society's approval shouldn't matter, but facing the bitter reality that it often does.

If mothering could be reduced to the instinctive gestures of the female gorilla at the zoo, then society would be correct in its assessment of it. We could all seek a surrogate. We could all find a good veterinarian to take over. We could all use technology to suckle our young before placing them back into the wild. *And many do.* But mothers know that the physical duties have another dimension, a higher plane in which they can teach their children their spiritual purpose and model a relationship with God. Its boundaries are much harder to see, however, because they stretch out into eternity, giving depth and meaning to the role others may trivialize.

An Eternal Perspective

If everyday reality demeans us as mothers, then eternal significance elevates us. But how are we able to catch a glimpse of our work's eternal implications? How do we crawl out from under the heavy indignities of child rearing and see the spiritual legacy beneath its labors?

One way we can gain an eternal perspective is by altering our attitudes toward physical work. Earlier in this chapter, we explored the daily demands on a mother—the constant saturation with material and practical tasks. These tasks need not take us away from God, but toward Him. Are the roles of maid, nurse, or teacher demeaning? Only if we are merely scrubbing floors, administering Band-Aids, or singing our ABCs. But maids, nurses, and teachers can also minister on a spiritual plane, the one that is much harder to see. A child's maid can bring order to chaotic space. A child's teacher can teach spiritual insights as well as the alphabet. A child's nurse can bind up a fear as quickly as a wound.

A mother with four young children once shared her formula for reaching the end of a day without suffering from insanity or exhaustion. She spoke of ready prayers, whispered from a kitchen sink or a disastrous playroom. She turned her heart toward God in the most spirit-less of tasks. In fact, the more mundane the chore, the more insistent the praise. She sang, prayed, worshiped, or hummed whenever the tasks seemed overwhelming. She recognized that God needs no appointment book. He can enter into our daily calendar with the slightest invitation, and He never breaks an appointment.

Of course, this same mom admitted that such prayer and praise was more an act of self-discipline, not an act of spontaneity. It took months before this spontaneous prayer and praise became a natural part of her exhausting day. And it started because she was never able to find the mythological "hour in prayer" that books and pastors told her about. She realized that interruptions were a standard rule of motherhood. One minor crisis blended into another, until the day became a system of damage control.

This is every mother's daily reality. Whether we have one child or six, whether we are wealthy or poor, whether we are twenty or forty—we all recognize the physical limitations of our day. Yet this mother turned these truths about chores and duties into reminders to pray. She would discipline her spirit to lean toward spiritual truths whenever the earthly tasks grew heavy. Such discipline retrains our attitudes until praise and worship become a natural response to each day, not merely another requirement of our schedule.

Most of us associate worship with a church service, the special time set aside for a congregation to sing and offer praise to God. But a mother's daily worship is something quite different. It comes in whispered refrains. A mother's worship seldom needs music and should be ready on the tongue at any moment. It is a silent and soulful communion with God when there is no time to kneel.

The Discipline of Rest

How else can we reposition our gaze toward heaven? What else can I do to find God in my very messy world? Certainly we all know the role self-discipline plays during our work hours, but what about our rest hours? Even the busiest of moms finds time to stop, but she doesn't always recognize it as rest time. Merely stopping our work and actually resting from it are two entirely different things. The longer I am a mother, the more I realize a fundamental truth about my day: *effective rest requires self-discipline.*

How many mothers try to refuel themselves every day with soap operas, eating, or popular magazines? How many of us saturate ourselves with consumer propaganda or empty entertainment? Poring over secular images, such as glossy magazine models or television plotlines, is not mere escapism; it may temporarily rest the body, but it chokes the spirit. If we as mothers are to reposition our gaze toward God, I am convinced we must train the mind to find rest and escape apart from the heavy influences of our world.

Of course it's easy to justify. I hear many mothers say that after a stressful day, they just want to escape, to collapse in front of the television. The need is legitimate: no one needs refueling as much as a mother. But handing a mother the remote control to refresh her mind and spirit is like giving a malnourished man a box of Twinkies. It will give temporary sustenance, but it does not truly nourish. How many times have I been exhausted, but then squandered my free time on something meaningless? When the kids wake from their naps, only *they* have been refreshed. I have not found *God* in the small gaps of time—only entertainment. It leaves me restless. It brings little peace.

What about silence? The spiritual benefits of walking, sleeping, reading, or meditating can bring us the silence we desperately need. Silence is rich. It smoothes out the day's wrinkles and points us to heaven. It chases away chaos and welcomes God into our home again. Silence must be invited. Unlike noise, it never demands to be heard. A mother must fight for it, for a home left to its own devices will always shout, never whisper.

I have often used the excuse that I cannot sleep during my child's nap time—there's simply too much to do. Nor could I possibly take a walk. Who will take care of the kids? And what do you mean, meditate on Scripture? My mind is too full already, and the house is far too noisy to concentrate.

In truth, there will always be another dish to wash, a logistical dilemma to solve, or a schedule that cannot budge. But if we look at our day, what will really be different if we take an hour to rest in complete stillness? Will our children be neglected? Will our husbands be angry? Will my life be richer or more fulfilling if I move from dawn till dusk without rest or silence? It is doubtful.

In fact, if I experiment for one week with the new formula, I make an astonishing discovery. My engine doesn't idle like it used to. My gaze has been turned away from the trivial. My spirit is turned toward God. The other members of the family feed off of my calmer spirit, and the entire mood of my home begins to turn from chaos to peace.

Rest is as vital to a mother's spirit as pure water is to a dehydrated body. Merely stopping our work is not the answer. It requires self-discipline and maturity to effectively refuel a mother's spirit.

A Mother's Spiritual Significance

If I have discovered anything in this discussion of a mother's worth, it is that her role requires consistent sacrifice and maturity.

Some years ago, my husband and I were entertaining one of his dearest friends, a trusted mentor and former teacher from my husband's high school days. My oldest daughter was two years old, and our second daughter was just an infant. During mealtime, I vaguely remember the typical dinner scenario: a pathetic display of toddler whining, infant whimpering, and a mother's frantic hospitality. Anyone who has raised little ones knows the dilemma. I felt like a complete failure as a hostess. I was sure our guest was uncomfortable—he was not a father himself—and I was certain that our efforts to entertain him were failing miserably.

Three days later, an unexpected letter arrived. It is a letter that I have kept in my daughter's baby book for several years and one that I have read countless times in moments of sheer exhaustion:

Dear Caroline,

When I was in the fourth grade, we lived in San Francisco where my mother was raising my brother and me by herself. She worked the night shift as a private duty registered nurse, then spent the daylight hours tending to our needs. There were days when her jobs became a twenty-four-hour obligation—like the day when I was too sick to attend school. By mid-morning, she had stabilized my condition. After she prepared lunch and cleaned the kitchen, she was really tired because other chores had kept her from sleeping the previous day. That adds up to many hours without sleep.

My healthy condition returned to the point that I was eager for some entertainment, so I asked my mom to play checkers with me. She explained that she was really exhausted, and suggested we play later that evening. Thinking only of myself, I said, "Well, let's play just one game now." Amazingly, she consented. Very soon I saw her head fall forward, then jerk upright as she struggled to maintain consciousness. It happened a number of times, but we finished the game.

It wasn't until years later that I realized how frequently my mom performed selfless acts like that for me and my brother. She did them so routinely and without comment that they passed without notice by me, a testimony to my mother's extraordinary love—and my constant self-preoccupation.

As we ate dinner Tuesday night, and I saw you quietly enduring as you tried to placate Whitney, comfort Brooke, please your husband, be a gracious hostess, and incidentally eat your dinner, I thought of my own mom—and all moms—and how parallel their roles are. When they are twenty-one, your children will not remember May 21st, and the countless other days on which you put them before yourself—but by then they will hopefully understand and appreciate your role of mother and what you did for them, even though they will never know it all.

Many remarkable moments rise from that letter: the image of a single mom choosing her son's pleasure over her own, a tired head drooping in sleep, and the mature insights of a grown man not only honoring his own mother but also encouraging an inexperienced one. At first it was humbling for me to see the parallel between her mature, daily self-sacrifice and my silly little dinner party, but as I read it over again, his words resonated with my spirit: *". . . a testimony to my mother's extraordinary love . . ."*

A wise letter indeed.

An Extraordinary Salary

Of course, there are as many ways to define the spiritual value of a mother's role as there are mothers. In every home, during every hour of the day, young mothers are laboring at a job for which there is little recognition.

It is astonishing to think of the vast workforce of silent laborers. Whether in sprawling estates, modest neighborhood tracts, urban apartments, or single rooms, mothers around the world are doing the work of God. We do not labor alone. One sacrificial act at a time, we are changing the world. Our bodies are nourishing newborns. Our self-control is teaching patience. Our voices are soothing fears. Our prayers are whispering hope. We all toil in private worlds, yet we share the same task.

Is there a price for such labor? The secret sacrifices of every mother cannot be tallied on a spreadsheet or time card. My children's grandmothers are now beginning to see the legacy of their own sacrifices so many years ago. Certainly, the benefits to their children and grandchildren outlasted any indignities they suffered in the process, but at the time, their world must have seemed very small.

How long must we really labor? Time gives us a few years to train our young children. The engine is heavy and slow-moving, but the distance isn't far. I'm sure I am closer than I think, but in my daily schedule, it feels I've barely started.

It is truly the work of God. And His work, not mine, changes my world.

It brings order to chaos.
It rescues me from exhaustion.
It sharpens my family's purpose.
It forgives human failure.
It softens pride.
It brings laughter to an ordinary day.
It holds me accountable.
It shapes my children's character.
It changes the whole world.

Food for Thought

Consider—

1. What flaws can both working mothers and stay-at-home mothers have in common?
2. Why is society's appraisal of mothering so mediocre?
3. What can the pregnancy analogy teach us about self-sacrifice?
4. What is the difference between *worth* and *self-worth*?
5. What is the difference between everyday reality and eternal reality?
6. What is the difference between stopping one's work and actually resting?

Reflect—

1. How do I try to justify my parenting lifestyle? What are the arguments I use to defend my sometimes selfish motives?
2. What are some examples of times when I feel my role as mother is devalued?
3. How can I refuel my body during times of exhaustion?

Chapter Two

Rushing to Wait:
The Paradox of a Mother's Time

$\int$ easons and sunsets. Clocks and calendars. History classes and hourglasses. Time's concrete, human symbols are our only means of explaining it, and each one must seem inadequate when we finally take our last breath. Nothing is so completely mysterious, so inherently valuable, yet so utterly incomprehensible as time. It is the one concept that children can only ask questions about, and adults can only pretend to understand. In fact, aside from the nature of God Himself, I cannot imagine anything as profound as the perpetual motion of eternity.

Time is not nearly so troubling to a child. At a young age, I learned that time was merely a nasty little enemy to be controlled whenever possible. When we are preschoolers, the concepts of bedtime, playtime, or any time can be reduced to childish requests: *Just-five-more-minutes, please*? and *Is it really time already*? Learning to read a clock, winning a relay race, and having all-night slumber parties (our grade school attempts to manipulate time) give us temporary control, or so we think. Of course, as children, we have not yet realized that our power over time is a complete sham: its effects are as involuntary as the beating of our childish heart, and its control is suffocating.

As a biblical studies student in college, I could never quite understand how the nature of God could be compatible with the chronological movement of time. I began to explore man's human analogies: multiple dimensions, linear history, Eastern cycles. But it only made me realize how incomplete my efforts were to understand it. I knew that God existed outside of my comprehension, but I still felt victimized somehow by time's effects. And then after an hour or so of mental pressure, class was dismissed and my young mind would look to the day's trivia for escape. My tiny scratches on the face of eternity seemed too small to matter and besides that, it made my head hurt.

A Mother's Clock

So we forget about time for a short while during our youth until suddenly motherhood introduces a strange new relationship with time. A mother discovers that time fights against itself with its inconsistent pulse and its simultaneous racing and pausing. It no longer ticks in neat little increments; it leaves us panting yet restless, frantic yet bored. No other role makes us as aware of this ironic, grinding engine called time.

Surely, pregnancy reminds us that we often cope with time by compartmentalizing it. We move from the first trimester to second and then to third, always waiting for the latest, greatest experience. *Have you felt the baby move? Are you showing yet? When are you due?* The pregnant mother often feels as though her current experience isn't quite rich enough. Oh yes, there's something more, something better on the way. These arbitrary milestones sometimes confuse the mother who simply wants to sit and be pregnant—no trimesters, no impending birth date, no fetal growth charts.

Oddly enough, after their babies are born, many women find their lives fall into two hemispheres: pre-birth and post-birth. Like the Western chronology B.C. and A.D., mothers package their memories on one side of the birth or the other, remembering the days before little Jimmy arrived or after baby Sarah was born. It seems our culture requires us to post our experiences in permanent marker on some fixed-yet-imaginary time line. Often we are caught in a time-coping system which, while worshiping the past and future, tends to undermine the present. The moment itself is ruined; the experience lost forever.

American mothers, in fact, have recently captured this paradox in their obsession with creating family memory books. We create elaborate timelines of family life and its milestones. We photograph obsessively. We hoard tickets, programs, and childhood pictures by the bagful. I have found myself spending weekends losing sleep and shooing the children away from our kitchen table full of supplies. Is there no greater irony than pasting photos of me and my cuddling children at the same time I'm slapping their hands as they reach up to admire them? There is certainly nothing inherently wrong with creating memorable scrapbooks, but it may do us well to examine our motives. Are we creating a mere symbol of our life at the expense of those same experiences we had hoped to capture?

Another time lesson we seem to have forgotten involves our inability to blend work and play. One of the elements of my personality requires me to have completed my work before I can enjoy play. My children, however (whose preschool minds I would love to transplant into my own), have no concept of work; if they do, then work *equals* play. I was especially struck by the profound differences between me and my daughter when she was two years old. Her ability to sit on the floor and be so busy doing absolutely nothing used to astonish me, but only because it had been so long since I had enjoyed childhood.

My own addiction to scheduling and my feelings of self-worth (which are artificially hung on specific achievements throughout the day, such as cleaning, organizing, and so forth) could hardly be set aside long enough to comfortably toss a ball at her feet or make silly faces in the mirror with her. Today, I spend so much of the day whipping time with my reins of duty that I often wonder where I want my horse to take me. Certainly not to another place. Certainly not to a better experience. Shouldn't I want to be right here, right now, to absorb the moment never to be duplicated? No, I'd rather find meaning in the meaningless, to waste what will never return.

The Busy American Mother

I can't imagine anything a toddler needs more than knowing where his mother is. If I sit in one spot for a time, watching and observing my son, he will run away for a time, peek around the corner, leave once more, and then march right back to find me again. My children love unhurried time. The simplicity, the calm, and the casual touch of their mother at rest brings them great pleasure. Their voices become quieter, and their play becomes relaxed and less frantic. In short, they are feeding off the contentment of their mother.

On the other side, I can't imagine anything a mother needs more than getting things done. I find myself plotting the puzzle pieces of the day, inserting empty spaces with duties as soon as the vacancy sign lights up. I usually do seven to eight things just while moving from kitchen to master bathroom: *wipe kitchen counter, pick up dirty rag, arbitrate a brief dispute, wipe nose with same dirty rag, take note of strange odor, listen to answering machine message, write message on toilet paper with lip liner while sitting on the potty. Voila!* I accomplished eight small tasks in less than three minutes.

The hurried mother is a self-made martyr, and

sometimes we think no other form of sacrifice carries as much status. Whether volunteering, attending a play group, working for a wage, or trying to exercise, we always have an agenda in front of us. And in the process, we love to wear the tired look. It makes us so much more admirable when our body language wears just the slightest touch of self-pity to every event or obligation. Most of the time, the tired look is legitimate, of course, but just in case we're feeling pretty good one day, it helps to evoke others' sympathy for our hard work.

I have also stopped trying to justify each activity because every one I choose always has a good reason attached to it. If we think our schedule will become lighter by eliminating our bad choices, a quick survey reveals that all the choices are good ones. *Should I quit work?* But then how will we pay the bills? *Should I cancel the date with my husband?* Our marriage needs to be a priority. *Should I stop teaching Sunday School?* It's only right that I take a part in ministry.

At times, such inventories are not too helpful in reducing our obligations. They may be used in an effort to reveal how great we are! How selfless and kind we have become! How indispensable we are to our church or employer or school! It seems rather ridiculous seen in this context, but how many of us have hidden motives much like these?

Vulnerable Warriors:
The Paradox of a Mother's Protection

ave you ever seen a mother lioness in a nature documentary? She is a remarkable lady. Poised and alert, she impresses me with her quiet strength. I never worry about her cubs for some reason. I wait for the footage of some bold intruder who brings her to her feet outside the den. I know there will be some scattered dust, perhaps a quick scuffle in the brush, but I never close my eyes. For some reason, no enemy ever harms the cubs. When I see her rise to her feet, I know the children are safe.

This sort of maternal instinct impresses me, probably because I feel so much weaker than the female lion who stands like a powerful sentinel at the door of her home. But the more I learn about my protective power, my own God-given instincts, the less I need to fear.

Where the lioness is protecting her children from physical intruders, Christian mothers feel the strain to provide both physical and spiritual protection. The physical protection is certainly instinctive, and we cannot overlook its importance. But a mother also creates a spiritual barrier between the world and her children, and she must be a vigilant guardian of their safety.

Two Homes, Two Worldviews

Perhaps you've met them before. You know, the Christian family who homeschools their children, has never owned a television, and refuses to read the newspaper? Mom's ten-year-old scissors do just fine for homemade haircuts, and the Bibles in the house double as history texts and literature books. The babies use cloth diapers and Mom breast-feeds until the next pregnancy. They grow their own vegetables.

Or perhaps you've met that *other* family. Their kids started preschool quite early. Their children's video collection is massive, and the toddlers know every Disney tune by heart. The children attend gymnastics, play group, or dance lessons, and Mom and Dad intend to get them involved in sports as soon as possible. Going to the theater for the first time is an automatic rite of passage on a child's third birthday, and Family Night consists of watching good ol' American sitcoms on television.

One family seems far too overprotective; the other seems oblivious to the influences of popular culture. What's most interesting about them is that you're likely to find both of these families sitting across the aisle from each other at your local church.

How Much Protection Should I Provide?

It doesn't take long before a mother realizes that she

must constantly determine which elements of the world are forbidden, which elements are necessary, and which are optional. Is protection restrictive? Biblical? And if the prevailing secular culture is everywhere, how do we teach our young children to process it?

When our children are infants, such concerns are irrelevant. Popular culture extends only so far as choosing which brand of stroller or diapers to buy. It is relatively easy to shelter our babies in mother's arms. One of the great comforts of having a newborn is the extraordinary protection a parent can provide her.

But as our children begin to grow, the tentacles of American culture and its media reach out very quickly into our homes. We must decide how much of it is appropriate and how much of it is off-limits entirely. We wonder whether the Cowardly Lion will frighten our toddler and whether a purple dinosaur has anything meaningful to say. We consider the affects of toys and cartoons, role models and teachers.

I remember when I first experienced such disturbing little tugs at my spirit. My one-year-old daughter (the first of my precious little ones) attended a birthday party for a four year old. All the preschoolers in attendance lined up on the couch to watch an animated feature film that was the centerpiece of the celebration. The film was grand and splashy, full of music and silliness. Yet it had a dark side to it, a side that revealed pain and suffering. As the animal characters endured all sorts of trials in between the laughs, I watched my daughter sitting there on the couch with the other children.

I knew my daughter was too young to process the themes of this complicated film, yet I couldn't help but feel that the images themselves, the inherent wickedness of real life, was seeping into her eyes that day. It bothered me.

Did I do anything about it? Of course not. My friends were there—Christian parents who were raising their children well. Was I to take her off that couch away from the other children? Was I to cover her eyes like a neurotic mother wanting to shelter a baby who was too young to understand anyway? I sat there and watched her chew her fingers and play with her toes. I sat there while she swayed to the music with the rest of the children.

I sat there.

What Boundaries Should I Choose?

Most of us often find that the stereotypical "sheltered" family I described earlier is a bit too eccentric for our tastes. They seem a little bohemian, a little too out-of-touch with the mainstream, and therefore odd. We are not too sure we want to align ourselves with such a radical lifestyle, so most of us choose a more comfortable parenting style. Rather than taking cues from biblical principles, our children's unique personalities, and our own moral instincts, we lean toward the parenting styles of those around us.

One of the ways we derive comfort and self-confidence as mothers is by copying the strategies of other mothers. Since our own mothers did not face quite the same blitz of popular culture that we face today, we tend to rely more on our peers to instruct us in matters of education and culture. It takes extraordinary courage to swim upstream.

In fact, most new mothers are insecure about defining the boundaries they set for their children. If I see eight out of ten mothers using a television as an appropriate educational tool for their preschoolers, then I will most likely do the same. Why? Because I find safety in conformity. If those other kids seem okay, then it must be safe. When I see dozens of toys in dozens of homes mimicking the characters and programs of American television, then it seems only natural that my own children should own some of them, too.

The day I chose to let my daughter watch a program against my tugging instincts—simply because it may have cost me some mild embarrassment in a social setting—should have warned me about the powerful effects of peer pressure among grown women. Isn't peer pressure a teenage issue, you say? If only it were.

Offensive and Defensive Parenting

While it may be the most comfortable, merely copying the families around us is not necessarily the best method of choosing a parenting strategy.

In countless discussions with other mothers, I've found that two different philosophies—each with their own important arguments—seem to dominate. I call them the *Offensive* and *Defensive* strategies, appropriate metaphors in the war for which we are training our children.

The Offensive strategy has its compelling arguments. The Offensive parent prides herself in being progressive and open-minded. Rather than isolating their children from the world, these parents believe children should experience life, live it without fear, and learn how to process it. Close friends need not be of similar faith; children can learn from different lifestyles, and perhaps even be an example to their friends. These parents may hesitate to give a flat-out "no" to a program or movie; instead they discuss issues openly without suggesting fear or judgment. Rather than attacking man-made systems of our day—whether politics, public education, or entertainment industries—one should work within them, and teach children the moral processing necessary to hold their ground.

Parents steeped in this kind of rhetoric seldom fear public education. They see the academic and social benefits for their children, and may quietly stereotype homeschooled children as socially stunted or dangerously sheltered. Christian parents with this philosophy use terms like "salt" and "light" to explain that children should share their faith openly within secular culture. They are proud of the fact that their children will grow up "well-rounded," sociable, and tolerant of others.

And who are the Defensive strategists? They love their children equally well. These parents desire to saturate their children in the love and protection of God's principles and His people. They are defending their children against the blows of the world. Defensive parents use whatever means necessary to delay exposure to violence and immorality. They value the innocence and purity of the children God has entrusted to them and retreat from images and activities that may compromise that purity.

Defensive parents are inherently distrustful of secular media and its influence. They are the last ones to use the Internet. They see little value in entertainment for its own sake and would rather spend time actively training their own children. Public education is not evil, but they believe that the ultimate responsibility for a child's education rests with his own parents. They may quietly stereotype the family next door as being far too permissive and headed for trouble. They are proud of the fact that their children will grow up morally grounded, compassionate, and secure.

So Which One Is Better?

Placed side by side, both strategies can seem reasonable, and we are careful not to judge the good intentions of either parent. But before we check off a box indicating which side we will choose (case closed), we must respect the complexity of this protection issue. I think what is at the core of this discussion is not whether or not we buy popular toys, watch cable television, or send our children to public schools. Like most issues of spiritual importance, it is much more complicated than compiling a blacklist of boycotted items. Such "quick fix" steps only address external behavior.

The very center of this dilemma involves spiritual discernment. For a mother to be an effective protector, she must evaluate the spiritual battlefield daily. She must understand both her children's strengths and vulnerabilities. And most importantly, she must know God very intimately. It is a frightening challenge to most of us, yet it is the only way to identify which area of the battlefield is safe and which contains deadly explosives.

The first, and more liberal, worldview that I described has many valid arguments. The emphasis on critical thinking and intellectual reasoning is admirable, yet it seems to ignore the vulnerability and innocence of a preschooler. The second worldview has a compassionate and protective instinct at its core, yet it may weaken under the scrutiny of a rebellious teenager. Neither one seems effective as a rigid parenting code from birth to adolescence.

In the fourth chapter of the Book of Galatians, the Apostle Paul explains how a Christian's instruction changes depending on one's spiritual maturity. It seems wise that the protection we provide our children should be proportional to their vulnerability. So in my own agonizing moments of maternal insecurity and confusion, I have found a few answers by watching the world through my child's eyes.

A Place for Simplicity

The first place to look, during our struggle of whether to protect or to release our children, is in their own world. Only in a toddler's world can we find a place so entirely simple yet astonishingly complex at the same time.

An infant's eyes are processing millions of pieces of information each day. A toddler's hands join his eyes, and the two become a machine at work. Adults must have forgotten how intensely we once learned about the world around us. What seems completely ordinary to us—water splashing in a basin, the flight of a wandering butterfly—is a magnificent discovery to a toddler. Theirs is a paradoxical world, indeed, where the simplest things become complex new discoveries.

Adults have become so desensitized to stimuli over time that we think that our children need the same grand flourishes to which we have grown accustomed. If we subtract the twenty or more years of sensory bombardment, we might be surprised to find a bit of naïve wonder at a spring bud, a round red balloon, or a brand-new package of paper-covered wax crayons.

Observe a two-hour segment of children's cable television. The advertisements are downright shameful. Our culture paints a child's world in noisy, vivid images, full of neon colors and obnoxious electronics. Gears turn, toys throb, and buttons release extravagant noises. If you're not sure about this, visit a friend's house with preschool children (perhaps your own?) and turn on every electronic toy in the house for five minutes. What sort of insanity might that provoke?

We have taken our adult world and imposed it on the young, twisting their own preferences until they beg for more, needing higher and higher forms of stimuli. Recently, I visited the home of a very mature young mother who was raising her seven-month-old son. I was puzzled by a peculiar object in the corner of the room, a plastic soda bottle with a rope attached to the neck. When I picked it up, the strange blue liquid in it flopped around like oil—a primitive contraption posing as a 1970s lava lamp. "What is *that*?" I asked. She replied calmly, "It's one of my homemade toys. Food coloring and cooking oil. Isn't it great?" My respect for her soared.

Sometimes our own desire for simplicity is innocently sabotaged by the well-meaning gifts of our family and friends. In fact, I'm just as guilty as most moms, buying the latest toys for every birthday party. To do less would seem rather stingy, heartless. Bring a plastic soda bottle to a baby shower? Heaven forbid! But before you throw out all your toys, realize that a life of simplicity can still tolerate plenty of gadgets in the house. We must remember that the objects themselves aren't the issue. But those same objects cannot replace natural discovery, human connections, and moral training.

I remember while planning for my four year old's birthday, I was feeling a bit of pressure. Do I rent out the local circus clown? What about prizes and games? How many children should I invite? Thinking that my daughter was dreaming of bounce houses and helicopter rides, I was humbled to hear her say, "Can my best friend and I play in the park? And a pink cake, please. With four candles. Daddy can come too."

A Naïve Land

One of the other ways that we can protect our young children is to respect the moral vulnerability of their first five years. While I have great respect for Christian parents who believe that they are training young soldiers for the battlefield, I do not believe that preschoolers are ready for war.

The first five years are tender ones in which children long for optimism and security. The preschool years should be full of lightness and hope, wonder and trust. It is a place where love and simplicity hold hands. It is a place where hugs are tight and laughter is long. It is a naïve land. A land of bright promise and astonishing trust.

A young child cannot yet process the moral complexities of our world. We often compromise their delicate worldview with cultural biases and adult themes. Even harmless preschool television tries to package weighty issues into trivial twenty-minute lessons. I observed two mornings of preschool television and recorded a frightening range of heavy themes: single-parent homes, self-esteem, sibling rivalry, greed, and anger management. Add a silly song and dance, and we parents hear only the merry chords from the other room—never the complexity. Absent from life experience and daily training, these themes become a silly one-act play, with the meaningful posing as the trivial. How can my three year old know the difference?

The military places strict health guidelines on their enlisted personnel. Any defect, whether genetic or accidental, may disqualify them. Before my children can ever be effective soldiers in the war, they must be healthy. And there is no better time to feed them, to strengthen them, or to protect them than in their first five years.

A Parent's World

So if we have explored a child's world and found that it is characterized by vulnerability and simplicity, what is a mother's world characterized by? We've already established who needs protecting. But another question must be: *Who is doing the protecting?*

If I am a soldier in battle, and it is my turn to sleep for a few hours, I want to know who is standing guard while I am not. Is he a casual soldier? Does he know how to recognize the enemy? What if he falls asleep? If mothers create the front line of defense for their children, what kind of eyesight do they have?

I am constantly amazed at how casually I've accepted the influence of secular culture on my own life. If I am lax about the effect of sexual, violent, or immoral images on my own life, then I am probably not as vigilant about the images my own children are exposed to. And like most Christians, it's easier for me to obsess about the corruption of Hollywood than to explore other cultural enemies. What about irresponsible laziness? Overindulging in shopping or recreation, alcohol or food? What about Western materialism or vanity? One need not own a television to succumb to these temptations.

One mistake we can all easily make is putting our own spiritual journey on hold while we busily tend to the moral needs of our children. We push the "pause" button on the VCR, thinking we'll get back to it later once we've sent our kids on their way toward moral success. It won't work. The spiritual life is never static. We are either moving forward or backward. I've heard women say things like, "My spiritual life is just stuck in neutral" or "I'm in a rut," but the truth is that any delay in progress means subtle-yet-certain decline.

Have you known parents who wait until the toddlers are in bed before indulging in activities which are otherwise "off-limits"? When the lights go off in the back bedrooms, we feel free to hack down the hedge of protection we've spent all day gardening for our children. For some parents it takes the form of questionable films, painful addictions, or irresponsible laziness. For other parents, the gossip starts freely flowing or selfish arguments surface. We have separated our lives into two spheres: the morally strict world of our children and the morally permissive world of their parents.

Without the steady attention first to our own moral choices, we are merely talkers, just powerful little rulemakers with very little credibility. I'm reminded of the preflight instructions that airline attendants give their passengers before take-off. "If you are accompanied by a child, make sure you put on your own oxygen mask first before assisting your child." What a wise application for ourselves. When all the adults in this country are gasping for breath, how can we expect to provide oxygen for our children?

The Rustle in the Grass

Finally, it seems that I must return to the little scene in which my one-year-old daughter innocently watched a film with the other children at a birthday party. It haunts me because it only tells a sad story, one that I've repeated throughout my parenting journey.

God has placed powerful instincts within mothers. Granted, sin can interfere with those divine tuggings and we hear about many mothers who have abandoned them altogether. But the "protective instinct" that we constantly hear of is no myth.

Some instincts are universal, like pulling our children close to us in a parking lot or feeling their foreheads at the first sign of a fever. Others are perfectly matched between mother and child—a mysterious and unspoken pairing between a child's greatest weakness and his mother's greatest protection. Only a mother knows her own child intimately. One child can be free to wander a backyard unaccompanied while another must be watched with an eagle's eye. One child sees a Halloween costume and giggles; another conjures up nightmares on contact. The years have brought me wisdom and understanding with my own little ones. The same principles may not work with the children next door.

One of the most powerful enemies of our own natural and protective instincts is the social influences at work around us. I wish I had had the bravery and wisdom to draw my little girl to my heart and dance away from the television screen that day. Not in some showy display of superiority or self-righteousness, but because my soul was restless. And a restless soul must be brought to peace.

I believe my own parents were at peace most days. I'm sure they would tell of some frightening doubts and prayer vigils during our teenage years. But they held to us tightly during our earliest years and gradually released us to the care of God. Plenty has been written about letting children gain independence and responsibility, *but the first few years are not the time to begin.* Whatever protection we can offer, whatever our eyes scan on the horizon, we must draw the little ones to us in a fierce show of bravery.

Like the video footage we see of a lioness in every nature documentary, we must hear the rustle in the grass. We must catch the scent of our children's natural enemy and feel the ground move beneath us long before he arrives. When he comes, there is a brief scramble for territory as choking dust fills the sky, and the cameraman gets tense. But in a moment, the fight is over, and we return to our patient vigil. There have been no casualties.

Food for Thought

Consider—

1. How do most parents choose a parenting strategy?
2. What is the difference between an offensive and a defensive approach to parenting?
3. What are some enemies of a child's simplicity? His moral vulnerability?

Reflect—

1. In what ways have I lacked courage in protecting my own children?
2. When it comes to the influence of popular culture, what are some areas of personal weakness?
3. What specific instincts do I have about my child? In what areas does he or she seem to have a weakness?

The Nursery and the Bedroom:

The Paradox of a Mother's Sexuality

She was eighteen and pregnant, a very young woman with a very old problem. Her sexual behavior, not unlike many young women her age, had brought her to this unhallowed place, and now she faced the reality of motherhood. She sat across the restaurant table from me and told me the news, blank-faced, desperate, snared. She was a student of mine, newly graduated with an academic record to envy, but a ten-dollar home pregnancy test had introduced a shocking new concept: sex and motherhood were made for each other.

Sex and motherhood? I could see it in her eyes. *When did the two converge?* A moment of passion concluded with a lifetime of parenting, and no amount of biology or sex education had ever hinted at the connection before. It seems so ridiculously obvious, this simple cause-and-effect relationship between sex and motherhood, yet we seldom see it coming, especially in our youth. This young girl thought she knew all the rules, but not until this moment did the game finally make sense.

Is It Passion or Procreation?

It's amazing that with such a clear-cut biological connection between sexual behavior and pregnancy, we still struggle to find the link between the role of mother and sexual partner. Young, unwed mothers are certainly not the only ones to discover that being a mother and being a sexual partner seem incompatible. Even in the most monogamous, loving marriage, the shift in role takes us by surprise. In truth, a mother's newly functional body seems to break the spell of sensuality, and we often wonder how we moved from exotic dancer to full-bellied mama so quickly. We lament the loss of our independent, sexual bodies and must exchange them for the utilitarian machines that they become.

Part of our awkwardness in reconciling the bedroom with the nursery is that everything about motherhood seems to work against our own femininity. If mothering is supposed to be the summit of womanhood, why does it seem to destroy everything about us that seems womanly? Breast milk, maternity wear, baby powder—none of these are found in one's boudoir, to be sure. And yet oddly that's where it all started.

In addition, the move from sexual performance to parenthood, we are told, is supposed to be a mature path, one that takes us to a higher level of intimacy with our mate. It sounds suspiciously like the men who explain to their single friends the effect marriage has had on their well-being: "Well . . . it's a *different* kind of happiness." Likewise, our intimacy changes to a different brand, and even the most devoted parents can sometimes look fondly back at the early days of marriage when intimacy sometimes meant a superficial roll in the hay. The good, sweaty romps didn't always have to be spiritual, and the after-sex conversations didn't have to end with, "We should do this again next month."

Of course, women are not the only ones who must process the shift in identity. A man, often expected to say that his wife is even more beautiful pregnant, may instead feel less than sexual toward her growing belly—and feel guilty about the aversion. He must miss the almost spiritual mystery of the female body, now blatantly utilitarian and hopelessly functional. Any territory that was once all his now intimately belongs to another person, and not only is he supposed to accept it, but *ooh* and *ahh* over the beauty of it all. And, unlike a woman, who at least replaces the lost intimacy with a profound link to her new baby, a man must merely sit and observe.

It's no wonder, then, that motherhood in all its feminine glory can rob us of the very thing that got us there. But while sexuality, by nature, seems the very opposite of motherhood, perhaps it is best to see them as healthy allies instead of bitter enemies. They offer an exceptional balance to our lives by keeping us from two extremes of the feminine identity.

The Harlot

The first extreme is found in the woman who defines herself only in terms of her sexual role. This may not be only one's performance or the act itself, but in the superficial trappings of external beauty or self-absorbed vanity. The women in ancient cultures who were raised to be royal harlots, living in harems, spending their days preparing for sheer nothingness were not wholly unlike many of us who have been taught somehow that one's sexuality is oneself. When our feminine identity becomes wholly external—and one need not be promiscuous to indulge in such fantasy—we have lost our value as women.

Much has been written of the media's crippling images of women and their narrow roles as harlots and pinups. But it is not only the men who have forced us there. When we see ourselves merely as sexual ornaments—even for our husbands—we bring a little microcosm of the world's flawed system into our own bedrooms. A preoccupation with our appearance, our flirtation with vanity, and our competitive desire to provoke envy among other women prevents us from finding our identity in Christ. We become private harlots, self-absorbed and superficial in our role as women.

The Madonna

But wait. Many Christian mothers, with a touch of self-righteousness, find that a preoccupation with their sexual identity is the least of their worries. Simply finding time to complete all the responsibilities of domestic life is enough to keep the harlot from surfacing. But as is common to many of us, we can also swing to the other extreme. The cult of the Madonna, and by that I mean clinging to the myth that motherhood is the apex of femininity, is both dangerous and inaccurate.

A woman's role as mother is no doubt significant. It is without question a God-given privilege and sobering responsibility, but it does not complete us. Our children do not eclipse our own identities, and the temptation to worship our own children can only take us further from God. The well-intentioned mother who sees herself only as martyr and Madonna will find herself struggling to survive when that role has faded. Also, what of the millions of women who, for any number of legitimate reasons, do not have children? Are they somehow less of a woman, less noble, or incapable of serving God?

This sort of obsessive identity-seeking falsely elevates us and seeks to bring glory to ourselves, even though we have convinced ourselves that we are only serving the children. It creates a kind of reverse vanity, an attitude that is surprisingly self-centered and competitive at its core. Furthermore, the abandonment of sexual pleasure hardly seems sinful; in fact, it can seem downright chaste. Yet even Scripture instructs marriage partners not to forfeit their physical pleasure.

Our mothering pose can alienate our husbands as we

begin to treat them more as children than partners. Am I giving my husband a list of chores and sending him off to bed? Does he become simply another family member in the maternal nest? The sexual partnership we formed before we became parents must not be abandoned while I serve my children.

It seems clear that when we fragment ourselves into female roles, clinging stubbornly to one or another, we are undermining the whole. Much like the purpose of Eden's garden, God's original design and intentions are perfect; our human leanings cause us to see those blueprints out of focus. The tendency to long for a child and then complain when he steals our fun is indicative of our entirely human response to two God-given roles.

A Feminine Alliance

How do we place the two in healthy balance? Do we pursue one over the other, or both at the same time? Neither. The starting point, as with all matters of human weakness, is to seek our identities first in Christ. The New Testament instructs us regarding the tension between earthly pursuits and spiritual responsibility. Our bodies live in a fallen world with all its trials, but we train our spirits to live outside of it.

If our identities are grounded in the spirit of God, then our earthly roles have inherent meaning and significance. Instead, we often try to apply an external formula that says, "If you read your Bible first, then nurture the children, then satisfy your husband, you're doing what's right." We impose a rigid code that judges itself only by external behavior and doesn't address the inner motives of the heart. Of course, just because I've found my identity in Christ doesn't mean that my earthly struggles disappear. But it does give me a starting point I can return to every time the world's expectations for women seem to tug me away from God.

Although they are separate, the body is never too far from the spirit. A spirit bent toward God will choose modesty over brazenness. A spirit bent toward God will nurture internal over external beauty. A spirit bent toward God will seek servanthood over recognition. Wherever the spirit rests, the body will find peace.

Food for Thought

Consider—

1. How do one's views of sexuality change after bearing children?
2. What losses must a man accept after the birth of his children?
3. What are the two extremes of the female identity?

Reflect—

1. How has my sexual role changed since becoming a mother?
2. To which feminine extreme am I most tempted to lean? How do the media, my upbringing, and even my husband tend to push me one way or another?
3. What are some ways I can bring biblical balance to my sexual identity?

Sin and Grace:
The Paradox of a Mother's Humanity

I have fifteen minutes left of my Sunday morning to complete the impossible. I have to dress three younger-than-average children in three better-than-average outfits in world record time. I need to find our Bibles, the Sunday School lesson, and my car keys. I should apply some lipstick. I need to buckle, tie, or coerce six different shoes onto six different feet. I need to—*what was it now?*—dump six different cans of food into the Crock-Pot, so that upon return from church, the house will smell extraordinary. Is the diaper bag stocked? Which reminds me—I really need to pee. Oh, and did I mention I am supposed to spend thirty minutes in prayer to prepare my heart for worship?

The Martyr's Excuses

On a morning that should elicit my most focused communion with Christ, my sinful impulses are spilling out all over the place. My husband and I slither into our seats among the congregation and take our first prolonged breath of the morning. The stream-of-consciousness thought patterns are dominating my head. *The piano is too loud my hair is too frumpy where is my*

*daughter's teacher did I make enough chili why doesn't
my husband put his arm around me during the service
the lady behind me can't sing I just can't concentrate
what time is it my shoes look stupid I feel like I'm falling
asleep . . .*

These images of a Sunday morning experience are
not mere fiction. We can call it normal, we can call it
life, but we can also call it sin. The nearly impossible
task of "preparing one's heart for worship" makes us
dismiss our failings with excuses: the morning is just too
short, the kids are just too young, I'm just too tired, or
God understands. And yet despite those excuses—which
sound so valid on a martyr's tongue—there is nothing in
our own words that can rescue us from our sin.
Motherhood may demand spiritual maturity, yet it also
sabotages it at every turn. As we have explored earlier, a
mother's earthly responsibilities are in constant conflict
with her divine role. Certainly a Sunday morning captures on film the irony in such words as, "GET YOUR
BUTT IN THE CAR—WE'RE GOING TO WOR-
SHIP GOD!"

We find the chronic contrast—between our sinful
humanity and God's divine purpose—shamefully
exposed during our acts of parenting. Before we have
children our home is intensely private. Our sin is
wickedly personal. As a single person (and even as a
spouse to some degree), we can hide our failings with a
bit more finesse and secrecy. We can reveal our humanity

in small doses if we wish, veiling our selfishness and flaws as we choose. But wait until children arrive.

Indecent Exposure

No role brings such daily accountability as being someone's mother. Of course, this transition happens slowly. When I had my first child, I remember being relieved that during her first year of life, I could still pretty much live in private. If I really wanted to, I could still eat a whole row of cookies right in front of her with no explanations required. During her long and precious infant naps, I could spend an hour flipping through day-time television with my remote control, take a thirty-minute shower, gossip on the telephone, or curse out loud if I really wanted to. Even when she was awake, the view from her infant seat afforded her no particular judgment, and most days I still felt I could hide my less-than-admirable moments. She was a constant presence, yes, but one that allowed my secret failings.

Today, the level of accountability has increased ten-fold. A five year old becomes the inevitable household spy and keeper-of-rules. Her innocent questions shine a painfully bright beacon on my sinful acts. Every empty show that I watch, every compromising phone conversation, and every less-than-honest comment betrays my humanity. A two year old runs to me when I cry, telling me *It's okay, Mommy. Why you sad?* until I can no longer nurse my self-pity. I must sneak for myself any food they are not allowed to eat, and I must do my own chores before I can make a list of theirs. How many times have they turned the corner to find Mom in guilty poses of selfishness or indulgence? How many lessons have I been forced to give them, not prompted by their own disobedience, but their mother's?

There is something even more troubling than this. Even if we are successful in disguising our sin or reining our tongues ("Please, dear, not in front of the children"), we are unable to disguise our hearts. Henry Ward Beecher in 1859 said, "mother's heart is the child's schoolroom." A parent who begins to "clean up his language" for the children may have a clean vocabulary but a profane heart. A mother who whispers words of criticism into the phone cannot lower the volume of her bitterness. A husband and wife who think they fight only in private shout at each other with every silent stare. Superficial acts of righteousness can never hide our internal flaws. The spirit of a child responds to our sin intuitively, and in this sense, we can never escape her gaze.

The Sins of the Father

This intuitive observation that goes on between child and parent probably has much to do with the wicked repetition of sin from generation to generation. One needn't teach a child to sin, but a child who learns patterns of greed, addiction, anger, or vanity will find it

harder to seek redemption for behavior that to him, seems as natural as breathing. Old Testament accounts of generations affecting generations bring us a historical rearview mirror in which we see our sins repeated. But it's much easier to shake our heads in judgment at an Old Testament king's evil lineage than to face the sin in our own family history. We are pathetically sinful and completely debased, and we needn't be abusive or violent to recognize our human depravity.

Yet in such frail spirits, how are we supposed to teach our children about righteousness and grace? It seems hard to believe that God asks so much of us. It seems hard to believe that He would place families together so intimately that we can hardly move without spotting each other's frailty at every turn. The infant who cannot yet perceive a parent's sin changes quickly to a child who senses contradictions. That same child changes again to a teenager whose gaze exposes every dark shadow in our behavior.

A Model of Grace

This leads us to the crux of the problem. Secular moralists would have us believe we teach our children through our acts of righteousness. They say that by modeling good behavior, a child learns to do the same. And Christian parents quietly embrace the same philosophy. Go to church. Be honest. Work hard. Pray that the kids will follow our lead.

What we forget is that none of us is equipped to teach our children about righteousness. Teaching our children to "be good" is a desperately futile enterprise. A depressing notion? A fatalistic philosophy? Absolutely not. But consider the difference between righteousness and grace. *Every hour we spend teaching our children about God's grace is an hour that leads them to personal purity.* Perhaps we have clung to a false notion that only through acts of righteousness or perfection can a parent teach his children about God's grace. Nothing could be further from the truth. Of course, no one would say that the alcoholic abuser who embezzles funds and sleeps around is better equipped to teach his children about humanity. But when we are talking about grace, a parent's struggles are valuable lessons for his children. To disguise them—or worse yet, to deny them—nurtures a child's own mechanism for hiding his own sin problems rather than confessing them and depending on God's grace for his forgiveness and restoration.

Of course, those visible lessons must be age appropriate. A four year old can learn nothing from a parent's fit of rage or a drunken stupor, but he can learn from a parent who apologizes for not listening carefully or one who admits he is grouchy. An older teenager can learn from a mother's temptations, a father's greed, or an uncle's false pride. Teaching good character—and the grace that enables us to nurture it—involves visibly struggling in front of our children in simple, age-appro-

priate language. We do not expect our children to
process complex moral dilemmas, but allowing our
children a glimpse of adult humility or repentance is
an appropriate model. Since their vantage point affords
them a clear view into our weaknesses already, we have
no choice but to train them how to identify and
repent of their own inevitable sin through modeling
it ourselves.

Now we're faced with an even trickier situation. If
our children must learn independently how to deal with
their own humanity and sin, how do we separate our
behavior from theirs? Do we take credit for our children's good behavior and spiritual journey? If so, do we
also take responsibility for their miserable failures and
sinful choices? It's a very old dilemma.

A Fiery Competition

Let's look at a vicious yet unspoken competition
that exists among mothers, a competition more fiery
and intense than any sporting event could ever elicit. We
watch and snoop and spy almost daily, trying to com-
pare the behavior of our children with other families. At
the park, the friendly barbecue, the pool parties, and the
Sunday School classrooms, we spy on other children—
especially those of the same age as our own—and we
tally up the score.

We have an internal commentary about every act of
aggression or misbehavior. Her child pushed mine. *Look*

at how disrespectful her children are. My child pushed hers. *Did you see her antagonize my little girl?* We secretly delight in the misdeeds of other children because it makes our children look happier, better adjusted, better behaved. We likewise feel secret pride when the obedience of our own children appears superior to others'. What husband and wife haven't left a gathering of children without assessing all the parenting errors they observed? All the while, they are secretly defining their success against the backdrop of others' perceived failures, an artificial silhouette indeed.

My own struggle to define my family by our external behavior rather than our internal motives is born out of pride. A friend of mine once wisely stated that her main goal is not to teach her children to behave, but how to love God. The first goal may be merely a by-product of the second. How many of us find ourselves more concerned with the appearance of things than the spiritual core? How many mothers find secret pride in their children's good behavior—not because it reflects a child's heart for serving God, but because it reflects well on their parenting skills or self-discipline? It is a pose that is as old as the one practiced by the New Testament Pharisees.

Can That Child Really Be Mine?

Certainly, we seldom take into account a child's personal temperament. The parent who starts off with a near-perfect, compliant, and friendly firstborn cannot possibly understand why so-and-so's child is so unruly. Or why this little boy is so aggressive. Or why that little toddler is so sullen. He thinks himself a superior parent—maybe only subconsciously—until he has a second or third child who lands into his family with both feet kicking. *Uh oh.* The rules have changed. He looks up one day to find that others in the grocery store are shaking their heads at him, thinking him the permissive, inexperienced, or just-plain-lousy father. *It's all different now.*

It seems taking all the credit for our children's obedience and good naturedness is just as damaging as taking all the blame for their acts of sin. Even children have free will and a nasty sin nature. Molding our children's character and teaching them about grace and repentance is more a system of probabilities than a guarantee. No matter how precise we are in our spiritual training, no matter how vigilant our efforts, we do not bring our children into heaven with us. Certainly one of the lessons in this paradox of leadership and repentance is that every person must come to Christ's salvation on his own. Unlike the inclusiveness of medical insurance, a child is not listed as an automatic dependent on his parents' *Eternal Coverage.* They make choices. They are separate. They are human.

An Unlikely Teacher

But while so much is said about the ability of parents to influence and teach their children, not much is said of our children's ability to teach us. The web of moral interdependence within a family is astonishing. The adult who lives alone has little daily accountability and few natural motivators for building character and integrity. But the parent who realizes his life has become a living textbook for moral choices lives by a new standard. How many couples begin to rekindle their spiritual fire after having children? How many men reshape their priorities? How many women find new urgency in their prayer life? Our children become little beacons, guiding us to our mature conscience and revealing dark and hidden corners left dim from years of our own independent choices.

I've often thought about the choices I make for my young children and wonder why I can't choose them myself. *What's good for our children is good for us, too.* For example, I may regularly choose a balanced diet for my children, realizing that their development depends on the food we provide for them. Yet I will skip breakfast, eat ice cream out of the carton, or gobble french fries. I carefully monitor the television screen for violent or offensive images that may disrupt my children's moral development, but do I screen out similar images from my own consciousness?

The parent who sends his children to religious training without engaging in any himself will inevitably find a child who believes in a two-world system: one for children and one for adults. While there are some obvious differences between the two worlds, moral purity and spiritual progress are two areas where there should be little difference.

So, then, we teach our children the power of grace, while they remind us to protect ourselves from sin. It is a wonderfully symbiotic relationship, one that keeps both children and their parents moving toward repentance and self-discipline. And how do we let our children teach us? First, we must confront our own sin as swiftly as we confront our children's. It would be so much easier if God gave mothers "time-outs" or made us say, "I'm sorry" to an offended party. It would solve many problems if only we lost dessert or a favorite toy whenever we sinned. But God requires our repentance, the humble acknowledgment of our sin, and the conviction to turn away from it the next time.

No martyr's explanations will free us from our own sin. Motherhood's struggles can only humble us, never excuse us. Every frantic Sunday morning and every exhausting responsibility brings us to God's restoration, and we must let our children in on our astonishing little secret: all of us, adults and children alike, can only find purity through God.

Food for Thought

Consider—

1. What about parenting creates intense self-scrutiny?
2. What is the problem with simply altering or hiding behavior in the presence of children?
3. Besides good behavior, what can a parent model to his child?
4. What kind of competition exists between mothers?
5. Why should parents neither accept all the credit nor take all the blame for their child's actions?
6. What can we learn from our own children?

Reflect—

1. What sin or sins am I unsuccessfully hiding from my children?
2. What negative behavior or sinful patterns did I grow up seeing in my family? How can I work to combat those tendencies in my own family today?
3. What can I do to model grace and forgiveness to my children?
4. What rules do I provide for my children that I would also be wise to follow?

Chapter Eight

Childish Wisdom:
The Paradox of a Mother's Faith

*M*ommy, when will I die?"

It's a question that sideswiped me while I was folding laundry one warm summer day. *What did she ask?* It hardly seemed possible that a four year old could be thinking of such things. Maybe she overheard my long-distance conversations about the recent death of my grandmother. Perhaps the story we read in the Bible of the young girl whom Jesus brought back to life triggered some personal connection. Was it a spiritual turning point for her, or was it merely curiosity evoked by the image of the dead cat we found yesterday sprawled to the left of our front yard?

Whatever her reasons, she decided to ask the most profound of questions at the most ordinary of times: while folding T-shirts and towels. Whatever I told her seems irrelevant now. Perhaps I cleared my throat or paused too long for her to wait for an answer. Perhaps I told her not to worry about it or stumbled over some awkward response. But whatever my answer may have been, I remember being impacted by the free and casual way in which a child could ask such a grave and frightening question.

My daughter's blunt and innocent request for information illustrates some important truths about spiritual matters. Issues of faith and divinity are not limited to the realm of theologians or mystics, as we sometimes believe. The deepest spiritual questions are always the ones our children think of first. Their questions only startle us because they force us to confront our own spiritual answers. Certainly, the way a mother answers her children's spiritual questions reflects the strength of her own faith. When we answer our child's innocent questions about the nature of God or His divine plan for mankind, are we hurried or vague, weak or indifferent? Or are we bold and forthright, answering with the quickness of one who knows the truth?

My surprise at my daughter's question comes from spending far too many years removed from my own childlike faith. As adults, we tend to divide every issue into secular and spiritual realms. We address the tough questions with a long pause, careful reasoning, or a helpless shrug of our shoulders. We are not only skeptical about "easy" answers, but we sometimes want to dismiss them as ignorant or superficial.

When one of my students asks me what religion I am, I am embarrassed by how long it sometimes takes me to answer. My mental computer kicks in, sorting and retrieving, processing data like a silicon chip. I'm afraid to speak too bluntly for fear of sounding too fundamental, overly eager, or brainwashed. This troubling fear of how the world views my spiritual walk tells me what I need to know: the simplicity of the Gospel message is clear enough for even a child to comprehend, but the world's opposition complicates my theology and tempts me to feel ashamed of its straightforward answers.

In training my children, I have to stop and reaffirm some fundamental truths as I face their questions. I know that the Bible is both trustworthy and applicable to contemporary life. I know that my children need the sturdy truths of Scripture to bolster them against the windy ideologies blowing across their minds day in and day out. I know that the wisdom of God is far superior to the wisdom of man. Then why should I be afraid of the straightforward answers?

The Faith of a Child

First of all, we forget that what may seem far too simple for a skeptic's mind to accept, our children receive with their whole heart. Free from years of cynical thinking, free to see God far more clearly than we, a child's heart seems closest to God's original intentions for mankind. True, our child is fully human, complete with a nasty sin nature that hardly breathes its first breath before kicking in with a noisy, put-me-first cry. But he has been barely removed from heaven, formed in the mind of God before the foundation of the world, and just recently dropped into Adam's world.

When my child asks when she will die, she has no

skeptic's motive; she isn't bracing herself for a two-hour discussion. She is ready to hear the truth and go back to her playtime. This perspective is extremely valuable to us as parents, who have lost some of the simple faith we relied on in the early moments of our conversion. To join with our children in discovering the direct Gospel message (*"Jesus loves me, this I know"*) is the rich spiritual reward of training them.

Of course, the skeptic would say that children will embrace any ideology—not just sound ones. A child who learns the rhetoric of racism or violence, dishonesty or heresy, will naturally grow to practice it unless his environment shifts. But this argument does not discredit childlike faith—only the false ideologies that prey on it. In fact, a child's willingness to believe anything brings us to the crux of raising spiritual children: it's not *whether* they will believe something to be true, but *what*.

Drowning in Relativism

I've nurtured a similar discussion in my high school honors writing class with interesting reactions. Many students tell me that no public school should embrace one particular worldview. Since no one ideology is superior to another, we shouldn't point to any absolute truth, and students should be allowed to see them all as equal. It sounds so very polite and so very logical.

I point out, however, that such a perspective is a blatant contradiction of what the schools hope to achieve:

the belief that all things are relative is, in fact, a *specific* ideology. A "neutral" worldview is not only impossible, but crippling. While many think that such open-ended philosophy frees children from narrow-mindedness, it actually leaves them flailing—and often drowning—in a frightening sea of unknowns. One must *always* choose, always sift through truth and error. Relativism is not a realistic option, simply an intellectual cop-out. So then, our vital role as parents demands that we provide not only direct answers, but the right ones.

Our children are certainly empowered by the strength of absolute truth. Unlike the stock Santa Claus lie, which merely provides them a few years of amusement, our direct answers about God give them a lifetime of stability. This kind of talk drives the relativists crazy. Just like those high school students who believe no answer can be fundamentally right, relativists believe everyone chooses his own path based on the situation, and ethical dilemmas are continually up for debate. They hate the implications of absolute truth, and they can't accept the exclusivity of Christ or the demands He makes on those who follow Him.

When my daughter sings this old Sunday School song, I realize how discordant it sounds, paired with the song of our generation:

One door and only one,
and yet its sides are two.
I'm on the inside ,
On which side are you?

To the world, these simple words sound so mean-spirited and narrow. It's just vicious propaganda that teaches children there are the haves and the have-nots. What could be worse? Relativists would rewrite the lyrics to say:

Many doors, so many doors,
And yes you may choose two.
There is no right way,
It's all up to you.

Now there's a song that will really provide security and hope for our children.

Logical Foolishness

Another thing we learn from our children is that the world's reasoning is mere foolishness in the mind of God. In fact, our children's faith captures the profound message of God's plans for us more closely than the apologetics of the most accomplished theologian. The more we depend on our own reasoning and powers of analysis, the farther we move away from the simplicity of

God's grace. The Bible introduced this concept first, by placing the deepest of mysteries in the body of the baby Jesus, and by illustrating many times the superiority of a child's spirit: "Verily, I say unto you, Whosoever shall not receive the kingdom of God as a little child, he shall not enter therein" (Mark 10:15).

This is not to say that the training of our children lies in silly or superficial responses. Some of the weakest spiritual training comes from parents who have not taken the time themselves to study Scripture or appreciate the very real and profound nature of God Himself. A child will need more than references to little guardian angels, "The Man Upstairs," or a cardboard nativity set in the yard at Christmas to appreciate the full mystery and wonder of Jesus Christ. In fact, many parents wonder why their teenage children have lost interest in the church, only to discover that the trite, watered-down spirituality that they had been feeding their children becomes weak under the pressure of the growing questions and natural skepticism that accompanies adolescence.

Fundamental spiritual training involves a combination of lessons. For little ones, teaching Christian doctrine can mean answering questions like *Why did Jesus have to die?* or *What does forgiveness mean?* In the very early years, my children asked questions like *What does God look like?* or *Can I bring my truck to heaven?* While these requests can make us scramble for quick answers, they are appropriate starting points for teaching doctrinal truths.

Basic spiritual training can also introduce personal responsibility as we instruct them to clean up after themselves or offer simple apologies to others. Simple acts of service or compassion are other good ways to bring abstract principles into daily practice. The gift of mercy is not a natural bent for most children, let alone adults. Letting a little one help to wrap a gift or prepare a meal for someone else is a concrete way to introduce self-sacrifice.

What Do I Believe?

The key lies in whether we have discovered which straightforward answers are the truth, and which merely cover our own insecurities about God, eternity, and our relationship to them both. A child's intuition is fiercely sharp, and it takes very little time to recognize whether a parent is sharing a conviction or a cliché.

One of the most valuable things about my own spiritual training as a child was the independence my parents afforded me as I moved into adulthood. They trusted the truth of Scripture enough to allow me to explore the difficult questions. They allowed me time and space to test the evidence, both academically and personally, before transferring Christianity from the realm of "the family religion" to the realm of personal conviction.

Consider an analogy that perhaps illuminates this

concept. As a young man, my husband began the tennis training that eventually equipped him to become very competitive in the game. The fundamental aspects of playing tennis are relatively simple, and he readily accepted those fundamentals. Making solid contact with the ball, maintaining a sound grip, executing the proper physics of a serve—all these were critical in establishing himself as a player.

But as he grew older, to these same fundamentals were added some sophistication and finesse. As a more mature competitor, both in age and experience, he learned to delve deeper into the game's complexities and relied on advanced study and practice in order to progress. In the same way, we are entrusted as parents to teach the fundamentals of Scripture to our children, giving them the easy answers that we know are true.

My husband never abandoned the basics during his training; in fact, the "feel" of the game relied entirely on the sensible early training he had received as a child. Likewise, we must watch our children's progress carefully, giving them age-appropriate biblical instruction, but always returning to the fundamentals. Then, as they mature, they understand both the absolutes and the complexities of God's message, having been trained to defend their faith and relax in it at the same time.

Motherhood affords us the privilege of drawing from both wells: faith and reason. Our own growth requires mature study, but our children require simplicity.

If we can answer our children with conviction when they ask us about life and death, if we can be bold enough to accept the simplicity of God's plan, and if we can give our children room to test these truths for themselves, then we have begun the sort of spiritual training that will equip them for a lifetime of faith and service to God.

As in most seemingly incompatible pairs, the paradox of childish wisdom certainly astounds me. The profoundly simple message of the Gospel treats both children and adults to the same great truths. Of course, my daughter's questions will change over time. The simple questions will become profound, and the profound ones will become simple, depending on her age, her level of intelligence, and her reasons for asking them. But as I follow her journey toward spiritual maturity, the one thing I discover is that the answers are always the same.

For both of us.

Food for Thought

Consider—

1. How do children generally approach spiritual matters?
2. What is the tension between relativism and Christian truth?
3. What benefit do children receive from hearing firm spiritual answers?
4. How should spiritual training adapt to our maturing child?
5. What can the tennis analogy teach us about spiritual training?

Reflect—

1. What was it about my own spiritual training as a child that made me feel comfortable? Confused? Explain.
2. How do I tend to react to my own children's questions about God? Are there any questions I might find difficult to answer?
3. Am I struggling with my own faith? If so, how can I nurture it?

Chapter Nine

Living in Heaven and on Earth:

The Paradox of a Mother's Treasures

*As he came forth of his mother's womb, naked shall he
return to go as he came, and shall take nothing of his
labor, which he may carry away in his hand. And this also
is a sore evil, that in all points as he came, so shall he go:
and what profit hath he that hath labored for the wind?*

(Ecc. 5: 15-16)

The writer of Ecclesiastes is a powerful philosopher and a persuasive artist. He must have pictured my little girl as she entered this world, slick and muddy looking, with only the blueprint of God to invite her to this place. All the worldly pursuits that fill her days from birth to death will eventually decay, and when she returns to God at the end of her life, it will seem only a moment has passed. That little newborn is an accurate spiritual metaphor for all of us: empty-handed, unadorned, and utterly helpless.

The Book of Ecclesiastes makes me ask the question: *What am I really striving for?* Is the earth's gravitational pull so strong that I live each day merely "laboring for the wind"? The words illustrate a truth about the human condition, especially when we consider the ways we scrape and claw for what is temporary while ignoring what is eternal. Its universal truth becomes apparent in our own lives: *the tighter we hold on to the things of the world, the harder it is to find the things of God*.

No set of opposites is more significant than the one that puts two contrasting worldviews into focus: the *world's perspective*, which asks us to value earthly treasures, and *God's perspective*, which asks us to store our treasures in heaven. The world's valuables are inherently useless for eternity. And lest we think that God's treasures have value only for the afterlife, we recognize their power to change our daily lives as well.

What Do We Cherish?

What is a treasure exactly? Is it something one might find buried in an ancient chest? Or perhaps a valuable object hidden in a locked safe? Maybe it's a collection of rare artifacts or a family's cherished heirlooms.

If one were to ask a stranger to define the word *treasure*, he would most likely find some interesting answers. For some, it may be tangible possessions such as valuable jewels, houses, or sentimental objects. For others it may be abstractions like youth or pride, intelligence or beauty. And for still others, it might be something they hold dear like their children and families.

The Bible speaks of storing our treasures in heaven,

for there they are beyond the reach of Earth's dust and decay. "Lay not up for yourselves treasures upon earth, where moth and rust doth corrupt, and where thieves break through and steal. But lay up for yourselves treasures in heaven, where neither moth nor rust doth corrupt, and where thieves do not break through nor steal. For where your treasure is, there will your heart be also" (Matt. 6:19-21).

The biblical images of moths and rust in that passage are strangely violent. Moths destroy that which is somewhat fragile: our wispy, superficial treasures. Some treasures have the vulnerability of old garments; they simply cannot last. Rust, on the other hand, destroys that which seems indestructible: our firm, more substantial treasures. Regardless of whether our treasure is made of delicate cloth or sturdy iron, no earthly idol can withstand the corruption of this world's inevitable decay.

It is important to recognize, however, that many of our earthly treasures are also highly valued by God. Just because we show great devotion to our children, for example, doesn't necessarily mean that our devotion to God is somehow compromised. Our children are extraordinary gifts from heaven itself. They give value and beauty to this world while leading us toward spiritual maturity.

We can certainly enjoy other earthly treasures as well. Owning and enjoying material blessings or valuing the memories and heirlooms within our homes doesn't automatically corrupt our Christian journey. Pursuing an education or saving for retirement doesn't make us slaves to this world. These are by-products of living in a physical place, one that requires some material attention. Plenty of God's blessings can be celebrated and enjoyed freely.

But regardless of my collection of valuables, I must ask myself the same significant question each day: *Toward which treasure does my heart lean the most?* The more strength I exert while gripping tightly to the things of this world, the less strength will be left in my hands to clutch the things of God. And at the end of our lives, the things of God are all that really matters.

Earth's Gravitational Pull

It might be wise to start by exploring the most obvious earthly treasures, the ones that dissolve into moth-eaten dust rather quickly. These treasures are the great superficial deceivers of our day, the things that easily rob us of what is significant. For many of us, some of the greatest struggles are not against evil demons or overtly wicked lifestyles, but against an increasingly superficial worldview.

And such superficiality is no longer subtle. When I picture this worldview, I think of the New York Stock Exchange, fraternity parties, and billion-dollar businessmen. I see giddy entertainment, the cosmetics industry, and the ridiculous antics of cable television. I reflect on shopping addictions and plastic surgery. We are a world of soap operas, white teeth, and dog therapists. As technology and a prosperous culture have given us more and more money and free time, we have scrambled to spend both of them on the most superficial things possible.

This same counterfeit worldview is heavily marketed to our children. We teach our children far more about pleasure and recreation in this country than we do about charity, self-sacrifice, or devotion to God. Without moral training or spiritual direction, a child can spend his first five years in a cheap carnival, a world with spinning electronic lights, giddy roller coasters, and plenty of pink cotton candy.

This kind of worldview may seem harmless, but a steady carnival diet creates severely malnourished children. While it appears bright and exciting, a world-view without God grows increasingly flat and one-dimensional. Like circus performances, circus life lasts only as long as the tents are pitched. Before long, the clowns grow tired, the arena seems noisy, and the animals make an awful mess. Life may shout and make wild gestures, but it is, in Shakespeare's words, "full of sound and fury, signifying nothing."

But, you may ask, isn't this getting a bit too serious? Aren't we being too critical of a child's only chance to enjoy the world? Aren't children supposed to be having fun?

Absolutely. I'm in no way suggesting that we return

to a stiff world of sobriety and discipline that hardens the spirit or discourages laughter. This was the world that affected many of our grandparents, making them fearful, judgmental, and always suspicious of pleasure. However, laughter and simplicity are worlds away from indulgence and excess. Our children are watching us every day, learning the most important lessons of their world during the first five years of life. They learn from us the definitions of pleasure and self-control, relaxation and work. They watch our own idols and learn what to worship. They begin to recognize what is lasting and what is temporary.

While most of us know that the sinful excesses of our culture can gradually swallow our sense of God, we still flirt daily with the world's culture. On most days, I choose the superficial over the spiritual in a flurry to pursue things that have no real value. Does my haircut really matter that much? Will my dishes or wardrobe or house colors really be that important at the end of my life? Who will remember what I served at my daughter's birthday party? While I would never label these external pursuits as my "treasures," taken collectively—as one big, meaningless whole—they can begin to eclipse the value of my Heavenly Father.

A Spiritual Response to an Earthly Reality

It becomes clear, then, that superficial treasures are indeed costly. They gradually rob us of our purpose and our spiritual direction, and the older we get, the emptier they become. In short, temporary treasures are things that turn attention to ourselves and away from God.

So, then, how do we build our treasures in heaven? How do we teach our children about spiritual value in the midst of a superficial society? Certainly eternal significance is reflected in what we teach and model to our children beyond the daily physical tasks.

One way to reposition our gaze toward heaven and away from earth is through our acts of service. Consider the difference between the world's model of hospitality and Christ's model of servanthood. The world, with its increasingly competitive and hostile environment, has abandoned the art of true hospitality. The best it has to offer is a Martha Stewart counterfeit, a polite but efficient hostess who offers clean towels and some nifty *hors d'oeuvres*. Many times these are earthly concerns—not spiritual ones. Certainly, most tasks are essential to a home's efficiency, but others are simply acts of pride. The superficial fussing, cleaning, and showcasing of our homes can very quickly turn to idolatry, and it degrades our spiritual legacy. Such acts, when motivated by pride, have very little to do with spiritual hospitality.

The hospitality of Christ demands much more: a spiritual openness, a readiness to sacrifice, and a place to wash others' feet. A child who sees his home as a father's trophy or a mother's idol is a child who will grow up entertaining others as a means for recognition.

However, a child who sees his home as a simple resting place for strangers, with no expectation of a returned favor, is a child who will live his life as a gracious, spiritual host for the world.

Perhaps another way we teach our children what is valuable is by acknowledging eternal—not external—beauty. The hours I spent looking into the unattractive faces at local convalescent hospitals when I was young affected me more than I realized. A child who has never stroked an ugly hand, never smelled a foul urban mission, never hugged a broken body is a child who learns a distorted ideal of beauty. My parents' compassion and tolerance for others' imperfections reflected their respect for human life. Spiritual significance is not taught only during family devotions, but in practically serving the needs of all humanity—even the most broken or unattractive.

There is no question that we also develop a spiritual legacy in our daily communion with God. The prayers of my own mother represent our family's spiritual foundation. Often unknown to her own children, seldom mentioned, and rarely discussed, my mother's prayers became the sturdy foundation of our childhood. They were not some magic formula used to manipulate God's mind or guarantee safety, but her prayers restored her own relationship with God and refueled her spiritual body. While prayer can be a powerful, concentrated time of intercession on one's knees, it can also be far less formal. The whispers of hope that hang ready on the tongue, the words of praise for simple, everyday blessings, or a meditative spirit during moments of crisis—these can all model the kind of spiritual legacy we hope to leave our children.

While my mother's prayers may have seemed subdued compared to the loud, boisterous prayers of my grandmother, many generations will hear the rhythmic sound and feel the impact of both those shouts and whispers. Will my children and grandchildren replay sensory images they remember of my own prayer life? Are we adding a chapter to the spiritual legacy of our families, or has the ink run dry on history's pen?

Releasing the Earth

Releasing our earthly treasures does not happen easily, and apart from God, it cannot happen at all. Some of us try to physically pry our fingers off of earthly treasures, regardless of whether they are counterfeit jewels like materialism or vanity, or valuable treasures like priceless children. This can only become a temporary release because as soon as we see them slipping away, our panic makes us grab them all the tighter. It is the human condition, not a spiritual one. Others may try to punish themselves for chasing worldly pursuits, relying on legalistic rules or sheer willpower to release harmful obsessions.

Both of these strategies place the focus of control on

man himself. These methods are destined to fail. I once saw a film where a drowning man died as he struggled to free himself from his heavy boots; a life raft floated several feet from where he drowned. He was so focused on the heavy boots, he forget to hang on to his salvation.

Our strength, our energies must be taken up in eternal significance—things such as communion with God, personal purity, genuine rest, cheerful worship, and an eternal perspective. These become my lifelines, and God is ready to supply them. As a result, I will have less time to pursue the trivial, and I will be nurturing treasures in heaven.

Where Neither Moth nor Rust Corrupt

But here is the grand finale—the perfect message of hope for all who believe in God's message to mankind.

When we return to God, as naked as the day we were born, will we have labored for the wind? A worldview with God at the center is not a counterfeit. It contains no bells or whistles to deceive us. It isn't a mere carnival ride where we hang on tight while the giddy world spins around us in artificial colors. It doesn't sell our children cheap toys or offer them daily, unsatisfying tufts of cotton candy. The treasures of His love are enduring and unaffected by time or decay. They last for an eternity.

When I have raced through this life with astonishing

speed, I will look at the future and the past differently. I may see a paradoxical past that was not nearly so important, yet more important than I believed. I may see that the moths and the rust have already devoured many of my valuables, rendering them useless. I may find that my hands are nearly paralyzed from gripping the world so tightly. In a world with little substance, I may find that my little idols have gathered dust in the corner of my life, looking cheap and powerless.

But then again, I may also see a future that reflects lasting dividends on some wise investments. I hope to see a Heavenly Father who knows me intimately after years of fellowship. I hope to see children who have not been lured by counterfeits. In the final days of my life, I hope to remember a life of eternal purpose and spiritual substance. My hands will be strengthened—not paralyzed—by gripping the things of God. The future reflects what I have always known in the past: any investment in Christ has permanent value.

Our children know our hearts. They absorb our values and recognize our life's treasures, whether subtle or exaggerated. Where will we tell them to look? In whose treasure chest will they find their most important valuables? On some days they will find me trying to polish my most tarnished pieces. But over time, only the things of Christ will shine as gold.

Food for Thought

Consider—

1. What are two kinds of earthly treasures?
2. What are some marks of a superficial worldview? How does it affect our children?
3. What is the difference between the world's hospitality and spiritual hospitality?
4. What are some things mothers can do to release their grip on earthly treasures?

Reflect—

1. What sorts of things attract me to this world?
2. How can I build a spiritual legacy for my children?
3. What are some practical ways I can change my focus from earth to heaven?

A Half Day's Worth of Shout

A bright room dots
early Spring's deep midnight
with light

You have called me here.

Pain hangs about the room
its inconsistent pulse in my veins
and the noiseless canopy
quivers in bold rhythm

A half day's worth of shout succumbs
to a second's worth of hush
before you suck silence
into your lungs
and return it screaming
and your wet, pale-ish skin
holds the light for a flash

Our voyage has left us shocked

Love's ocean
has swallowed me
though I have not yet learned how to swim

Chapter Ten

Fearful Courage:
The Paradox of a Mother's Love

"Daaaadddy!" My toddler's wails break open the deep quiet of night. I hear my husband stir and he leaves the warmth of our bed to crouch in the chilly hallway by her door. Will the cries last for long, or is it merely a brief nightmare? She cries again. His shadow steps into her room and fades away. I hear the rustle of bedclothes, a brief pause, and then her quivering voice grows still.

She has been rescued.

To a child, fears have their way of creeping into bedtime stories or dark caverns beneath the bed. As children, we shake them off with Daddy's trip to our bedside after a midnight dream.

As teenagers, our fears shift from imaginary monsters to the demons of the unknown: higher education, marriage, independence. As we respond to each unknown with a firm decision, the fears begin to dissolve. But later, as we grow into parents, the fear that we had been able to shake off during our youth now becomes a very real enemy who takes up permanent residence in our hearts.

Love Is a Risky Business

How can motherhood with all its loveliness and simple contentment be mocked by fear's quietly nagging, ever-present voice? It appears that love and fear are polar opposites, working in different camps, moving in separate circles. Yet, the two are inevitably locked together in a constant dialectic, one that plays out in a mother's head even when she sleeps. This very real tension—between a mother's protective love for her child and the accompanying fear that walks beside it—supports what parents have known all along: the stronger and deeper the love we experience for our children, the greater our vulnerability and the capacity we have for pain.

Childhood experience illustrates this principle. We own a toy; it means very little to us. As we toss it around, perhaps drag it behind us in the backyard, it brings us mild pleasure and enjoyment. Consequently, on the day it disappears we experience no grief, no sense of loss. The ratio of pleasure to value is proportional.

As we grow older, our ability to cherish things outside of ourselves grows stronger, and the powerful fear that accompanies love begins its gradual climb to the top of our emotional hierarchy. When we marry, we begin to trade the independence to which we've grown accustomed for a permanent alliance that affects us even when we are alone. Suddenly, our decisions—even the ones that once seemed insignificant—now have implications for another human being. Any break in that alliance, that trusted link, brings disorder. Marriage marks the process of risk and self-sacrifice that prepares us for the grand finale: parenthood.

Boot Camp Required

Perhaps this natural process of moving from freedom to responsibility accounts for some of the failure that arises when an unwed teenager attempts motherhood at the worst possible time—the height of her budding independence. The order is disrupted; she has had little time to comprehend the risks and self-sacrifice of mature love, and the baby becomes merely a novelty, a selfish trophy, rather than a child for whom every risk must be attempted and every pleasure relinquished.

Marriage is not only a support system for parenting; it serves as an essential boot camp for controlling our natural selfishness and often vain independence. It is no wonder, then, that God intended family life to proceed in a specific order.

The fear that a mother feels for her child—fear of a child's injury, death, and even independence—grows out of an even more mature, multidimensional, and protective love than the kind that joined her in marriage. It is at work in a mother's soul from the very beginnings of life, for the slightest lapse of time without feeling movement in a mother's womb brings a curtain of panic. Suddenly, this giddy event, this celebratory time, this casual business of motherhood becomes a risky business as well. The protective instinct—and its partner, fear—takes most women by surprise after years of independence.

I remember distinctly the moment this new definition of fear became clear to me. As a young, pregnant mother, I had been more practical than emotional about parenting, seeming to focus more on the responsibilities than the "warm fuzzies" of impending motherhood. But ten weeks after conception, a careless driver sent my car spinning down a local street, bringing me my first taste of the love-equals-fear formula. Gasping for air moments after the accident, I remember clutching my stomach and thinking *God, protect my baby.* I did not acknowledge the new strength of love, the unfamiliar wave of panic, until that moment.

Emotional Vulnerability

Our protective instincts may be natural, but let no one assume they are easy. From the hours we give birth, and even from conception, we have bartered with fear, trading our independence (that glorious fringe benefit of youth) for paranoia. An evening out with friends, a romantic weekend, a satisfying career, even a good night's sleep—all hopelessly ruined by separation from our children.

Of course, we can still laugh with our friends at lunch, we can still pretend that we are alone with our husbands, we may still nurture a career or involve ourselves with hobbies, but fear has taken up permanent residence in our minds no matter what we do to evict him. Our maternal impulses follow our children as they move about the world, and separation becomes impossible.

A woman's emotional vulnerability only grows stronger as the investment in her children increases. The giddy warmth I felt when my infant daughter smiled full into my face for the first time was soon replaced by even richer dividends. When we notice months of discipline finally ripening into good behavior or when we catch a glimpse of our child's spiritual awareness—those are the milestones that mark the pricelessness of our investment.

But as the satisfaction increases with each plateau my child reaches, so does the risk. The fears of motherhood may be obvious ones, but ones that we only entertain in private; the spoken words sound too ominous in our ear. It took weeks after my daughter's birth to even discuss sudden infant death syndrome with my husband. Any mother of a newborn baby knows the horrifying images she plays in her head, the secret, hollow emptiness in the stomach, and the haunting questions. Mothers find frightening gravity in news stories of child abuse and abduction because they intersect with her own hidden nightmares. These are the new costs of motherhood, and no one ever mentioned them at the baby showers or in the congratulatory letters and cards sent to the maternity ward. Motherhood is a risky business, perhaps the most frightening roulette game we will ever play.

I think that perhaps adoptive mothers experience love's gamble even sooner than most. Consider the risks an adoptive mother takes as she opens her heart (already raw from years of struggling to conceive) to receive a child. She must develop the extraordinary strength to tiptoe to the emotional edge of motherhood, waiting to see if all her love will find a resting place. The fear that her child will shrink back into the realm of sorrows is one that must be endured for months and even years before a child will ever sleep in her arms. In this way, she perhaps learns more quickly that the journey into motherhood is worth every single sleepless night, every physical trial, each emotional nightmare.

The Spiritual Risks

Our fears, of course, do not entertain only physical tragedy. There are certainly spiritual risks, especially those associated with adolescence. Every Christian mother faces the possibility of isolation and scorn from the very children she has nurtured for years. *Can't you just leave me alone, Mom?* The astonishing immaturity of a child who cannot see past his own needs cuts deep wounds into our own pride and sense of justice. *Why did I have to be born into this family?* And perhaps the most difficult trial of all—we risk seeing our children reject both God's instruction and His accompanying grace. *Maybe I just don't believe the same things as you and Dad.*

A mother's spiritual investment in her children's development far outweighs any earthly one, and it therefore carries the highest personal risk. Much has been written about a child's ultimate responsibility for his or her own spiritual direction, but it does little to soothe a mother who faces the sudden dismantling of her careful years of spiritual guidance.

Certainly, the risks that become a part of parenting remind us of the reality of living in an utterly fallen world: it cannot insulate us from sin and terror, selfishness and corruption. The best theological minds have tried to write on the subject of suffering and God's reasons for allowing it, and all of them still sound hollow to those who grieve over a lost or wandering child. God's hope can only guarantee freedom from spiritual sorrows—never earthly ones. Even the finest parents imaginable are vulnerable to the crushing sin (often not even their own) that can ruin their dreams at any moment.

And how do we release our fears? It doesn't happen naturally, and it doesn't happen apart from God. Do we fully realize that God gave birth to our children long before we did? Their destinies, their suffering, their purpose—I cannot control such things, even though I feel their effects deeply. After I have trained my children, fed them, washed the scrapes, stayed up nights, prayed for them, squeezed them tightly, and made plenty of mistakes, then I realize that whatever human love I have for

them is multiplied a million times in the heart of God.
" . . . perfect love casteth out fear" (1 John 4:18).

The Most Profound Gift

To focus only on the negative side of the love equation is to play the pessimist. The entire paradox is not stated: Love gives way to fear and we must protect ourselves. Instead, we have the privilege as mothers of experiencing the depth of God's love, and without the risk, we have not experienced our spiritual and emotional potential.

The joys that come as the by-product of this extraordinary step are not so easily categorized as the fears, for every mother has her own. Mine often come in concrete forms. I pray I will not forget the gentle breathing of my infant Whitney as she slept draped over my stomach in complete satisfaction. The awkward-yet-musical bang of an amateur instrument or the sweetish smell of Brooke's sleeping bald head, damp from my shoulder, are concrete images I cannot forget. The utter exhaustion of pushing Drew at birth into the hands of my obstetrician changed forever an otherwise quiet winter night. As a mother of preschool children, I do not know the joys that await me as they grow older. But every stage has its concrete imagery that bonds a mother to her children until death.

So, I ask myself, if this unavoidable paradox of love and fear must accompany motherhood, how do I focus on the joys without being consumed by its enemy? Considering the mothers whose worst fears have been realized—the woman who has had multiple miscarriages, the mother of a handicapped child, or the woman whose child has been abducted—they understand this paradox better than I. And perhaps I would have to ask them where to begin, for their struggles with fear must be greater than my own. But to me—a mother of three sturdy, near-perfect children—how do I live comfortably with the incredible risks?

I must begin with my foundation. It is a foundation that places my children in God's hands and not my own. It is a foundation that gives me eternal life through Jesus Christ. I have what many women do not—not through superiority or chance, but through the grace of God. There are no platitudes, no simplistic answers to the complexity of God's dealings with His people. However, He has given mothers the potential for offering the highest form of love to another human being—perhaps the closest thing to understanding His own unimaginable love for us.

In its imperfect way, the overwhelming love we have for our children is patterned after the plan God has for us. Jesus Christ, too, has risked His grace in exchange for a personal relationship with us. Make no mistake about it: this brand of love does not come from the selfish heart of man, who at every turn will choose personal reward over sacrifice. It comes from the heart of God the Father, who Himself modeled this love while watching His son Adam trample the very garden He had lovingly placed before His children.

It has not taken me long to realize that whatever fear accompanies this astounding journey into motherhood cannot eclipse the love God has placed within us. Whenever I hear the voice of fear, which is more often than I hoped, I turn my attention to simple days of grace, brown curls in the sun, fingers pointing at the marvels of creation, and little infant miracles. I turn my head away from the violence of my culture and embrace my babies in the quiet of the evening. When fear comes creeping down the hallway at night, I cry out for God to protect me.

And when my own wails in the night sound just like my daughter's, I can wait for God to crouch in the hallway, slip into my room, and quiet the desperation.

I've been rescued.

Food for Thought

Consider—

1. What are some emotional and spiritual risks associated with motherhood?
2. Are there any absolute guarantees in parenting? Explain.
3. How does faith in Christ affect our risk level as parents?

Reflect—

1. What are some of my own powerful joys of parenting? Powerful fears?
2. What aspects of my past make me more or less fearful of relationships?
3. How can I release control and better trust God for my child's future?

A Personal Note From the **Author**

Heart

I sat slumped at my computer many nights, hearing the soft clack, clack rhythm of the keyboard as I struggled with my identity, God's purpose for my life, and my children's future. I would leave that keyboard for six months at time, leaving the world of ideals to labor in the fields. I discovered it was much harder to live my life than to write about it.

It is frightening to realize that I have failed at every single principle in this book. To call myself an author would seem ridiculous, for I've always believed that authors must really know something. They speak wisdom at conventions and they sign books with authority. And what do I know? Days of failure and days of grace. That is all.

My credentials as a wise mother may be shaky. Those who know me will find a stranger at times on these pages, a writer whose words don't always match the reality of her home. But to find answers in the midst of failure is the work of God's grace.

Soul

What a model for mothers is found in Ephesians 5:1-2:

"Be imitators of God, therefore, as dearly loved children and live a life of love, just as Christ loved us and gave himself up for us as a fragrant offering and sacrifice to God" (NIV).

Mind

To explore these issues of motherhood further, consider reading the words of Lorraine Pintus, in *Diapers, Pacifiers, and Other Holy Things,* or Nancy Parker Brummett, in *It Takes a Home.*

Strength

The truths of this book are sometimes abstract. How do you and I put them into action? We must invite prayer into the corners of every day. We must rest our bodies. We must share our experiences with other women. We must record our failures and our victories, so that our children can learn from us. And when in doubt about our role as mothers, we must love our children to the end of the world.

> In Your arms, O Lord, there is *peace.*
> For every weary day, for every heavy task, there
> is *rest.*
>
> In Your presence, O Lord, there is a quiet *calm.*
> For every frantic hour, for every hurried chore,
> there is *silence.*
>
> In Your Word, O Lord, there is *truth.*
> For every lingering doubt, for every dark thought,
> there is *hope.*
>
> In Your purpose, O Lord, there is *life.*
> For every act of sacrifice, for every important duty,
> there is *love.*
>
> In the Father's holy name,
> Amen.

Caroline Ferd.